SELF DEFENCE
— FOR ALL —

GW00649713

SELF DEFENCE FOR ALL

FOR ALL

Fay Goodman

Photography by
Michael Chittleborough

A & C Black · London

First published in 1988 by
A & C Black (Publishers) Limited
35 Bedford Row, London WC1R 4JH

ISBN 0 7136 5587 9

Goodman, Fay
  Self defence.
  1. Self-defense
  I. Title   II. Chittleborough, Michael
  613.6'6   GV1111

  ISBN 0–7136–5587–9

Printed and bound in Great Britain by
Richard Clay (Chichester).

Acknowledgements

The Author would like to acknowledge and offer
special thanks to the following individuals who
kindly assisted in the preparation of this book by
being available as models or by making their
property available as a location for photography:
Pete Brady, Amesha Goodman, Ernie Goodman, Dik
Davis, Marion Davis, Pam Smith, Nigel Adams,
Geoff and Anne Brown, John Wisedale, James
Brazier, Ameena Ali, Lawrence Thomas, Alex
Thomas, Amanda Mansell, Dean Mansell, Pat and
Bill Mansell, Mick Blundell, Evette Smith, Bill
Smith, Gary Smith, Jan Ali, Tina Thomas, Fran
Burrows, Lea Beckenranger, Kate Goodall, Mr Lewis
(Manager, Royal Angus Hotel, Birmingham), West
Midlands Crime Prevention Division (Sheldon), Mr
Okimitsu Fuji (Honorary President of Shinto Ryu).

CONTENTS

(handwritten annotations) 1 HOUR

✱ ADVANCED SKILLS REQUIRED

INTRODUCTION

This book contains basic, practical self-defence techniques and useful advice on how to walk away from potentially dangerous situations without injury. The techniques have been taken from a martial art system called Shinto Ryu, a combination of elements derived from Karate, Aikido and Ju-jitsu. They can be used by *anyone* to his advantage. From personal experience I have found that senior citizens and sometimes children are not encouraged to take part in self-defence training and that only physically fit people are considered ideal students. However, it is often children, old age pensioners or small, inoffensive-looking people who are at high risk: attackers usually think twice before setting upon some-one who appears fairly able to defend himself.

'Self defence' simply means protecting yourself, family or friends from an aggressor or aggressors. (It is always important, of course, to be aware of your legal position in all instances, and this is discussed on pages 88–9.) The correct mental attitude to adopt in a critical self-defence situation is, 'What have I got to lose in trying?', and you may surprise yourself by what you can actually do. When life is threatened the body reacts quickly, due to the flow of adrenalin in the system, and it has been proved on many occasions that individuals have more than exceeded their usual speed and strength when in dangerous situations. For example, you may be capable of running only 50 metres at a good speed, but if you were being chased by a bull you would probably cover 100 metres or more at twice your normal speed! Similarly, if you were being pursued by a ferocious dog you could probably scale a wall 6 feet high without even thinking about it. There are many classic stories in which the most unlikely individual has warded off a prospective attacker by sheer determination and fighting spirit, having had no martial arts training whatsoever. It is also wrong to think that martial arts practitioners are exempt from danger. They may be well versed physically in their particular art, but when confronted by an unpleasant situation they may be unable to react. I cannot emphasise enough that at the end of the day it is up to you to adopt the correct mental attitude and to remember how, when and where to strike your assailant.

Self defence also means being able to walk away from a situation without injury and it is not always essential to use physical violence to achieve this. What is important, and preferable, is that you should try to talk your way out of an unnecessarily aggressive predicament. Just doing something unexpected, such as telling a joke or laughing, could make people see they are getting everything out of perspective and could help relax the situation. You should obviously be careful it does not have the reverse effect, so use common sense and a tactful approach. Helpful hints and advice will be given throughout the book to indicate how you can cope with different circumstances and how physical defence should be used only as a last resort and when there is no alternative.

So, bearing all this in mind, be positive about self defence, both from the mental and physical points of view. Don't feel you have to be fit, and of a certain stature, age, or weight, because most people can learn how to immobilise an attacker.

Throughout the book victims and attackers are, in the main, referred to individually as 'he'. This should, of course, be taken to mean 'he or she' where appropriate.

1

BASIC TECHNIQUES

When an individual defends himself he uses various parts of his body, such as his fists, fingers, elbows, knees and feet, as weapons. To make maximum use of these 'weapons' it is important to learn correctly how to form, for example, a fist and how to use hip momentum for strong impact.

Correct hip momentum involves rotating the hips and throwing the body weight in with the technique being executed. This means that instead of just the weight of your arm or leg being used, the whole of your body weight will be used against the opponent.

Try twisting one hip back and then bringing it forwards again, directing your trunk towards an imagined target and keeping your back straight. Avoid dropping your hip, as you will lose power. The time when the chosen technique should make an impact on the attacker is just as the hip reaches its maximum forward position. In other words, the two forces should strike simultaneously, not hip first and then technique (or vice versa).

To use hip momentum properly requires practice and possible supervision to show how it could be combined with the application of other techniques. Although it can play a key part in self defence to produce maximum impact, it is not paramount to people such as senior citizens who may be unable to use their bodies as effectively as more mobile individuals. Damage can still be caused to an aggressor by striking at vulnerable areas, such as the eyes or throat.

Hand techniques

Making a correct fist
First let's look at how to make a correct fist. Fold the fingers over to make an air-tight fist, locking the thumb on top. Try to avoid allowing your thumb to 'stick out': you could catch this in clothing or bend it back when punching and so do harm to yourself.

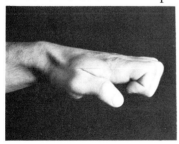 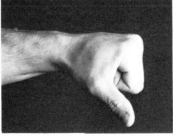 

1 When preparing to make a correct fist, fold your fingers tightly at the knuckles.

2 Always ensure that your thumb does not stick out when you have formed a fist.

3 Front view of a correct fist, with the wrist straight.

Practise making a fist and be aware of the fore-knuckles (the two knuckles next to the thumb as they run in line with the forearm) being prominent, because in certain techniques this is the area which will make contact with the aggressor. The wrist must be straight and *not bent*.

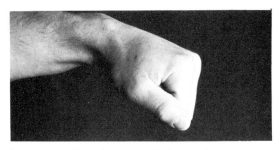 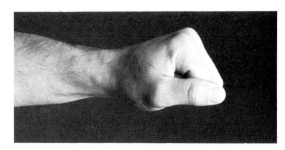

Incorrect fist: the wrist is bent downwards.   Incorrect fist: the wrist is bent upwards.

Another area of the fist which also is an effective weapon is shown below (hammer fist). This technique is usually used on side and downward attacks.

Hammer fist to the groin from a rear attack.

Inverted fist striking with the back of the knuckles.

Spear hand

The photograph below shows the hand made into a 'spear'. The fingers must be tightly pressed together, with the thumb locked in. If you fingers are weak, then there is a danger you will dislocate or break them, so take care to avoid 'splaying' your hand.

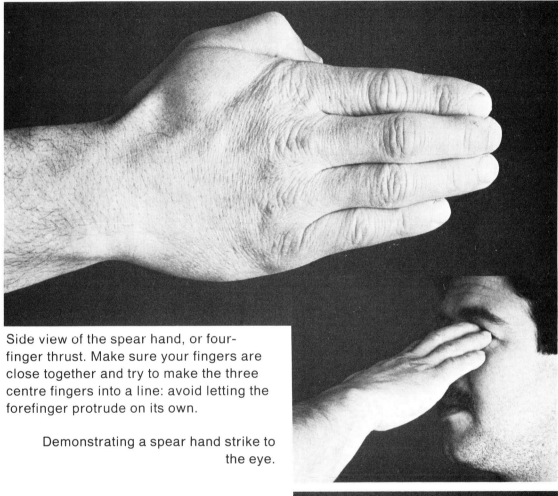

Side view of the spear hand, or four-finger thrust. Make sure your fingers are close together and try to make the three centre fingers into a line: avoid letting the forefinger protrude on its own.

Demonstrating a spear hand strike to the eye.

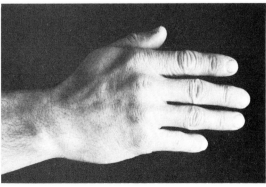

Incorrect spear hand. The fingers are splayed, making for an ineffective technique with no strength. It is important to wedge your fingers together to avoid dislocation on impact.

Finger and knuckles

Individual finger strikes may be used to an aggressor's eyes or pressure points. This may sound extremely unpleasant and it is, of course, very dangerous to strike at anyone's eyes. However, you must remember that in extreme circumstances it may be the only option available.

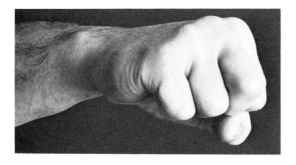

The foreknuckle is excellent for striking small vulnerable areas, such as the eyes. Apply the same principles as when making a fist, but push the middle knuckle forwards. Again, make sure your thumb is securely tucked underneath.

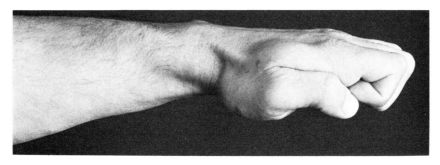

The knuckle strike: stop at the first stage of making a fist and lock your thumb in at the side.

Ridge hand and knife edge (side of the hand)

Both sides of the hand can be used effectively with blocking and striking techniques. If, for example, you were unable to use your fingers or knuckles because of arthritis, you could invert your hand to strike the aggressor's temple, nose, jaw, side of neck, collar bone, groin, etc. A selection of these strikes will be explained throughout the book in more detail.

Wrist

By bending the fingers well down you can make the top of the wrist very prominent and, again, effective when striking vulnerable areas. It can be used as a block, but the application is slightly more advanced than for the strike.

Palm heel

The hand must be bent well back (see fig. 3) to make the palm prominent and effective for a strike to the face area, i.e. nose. This is a good blocking technique, too.

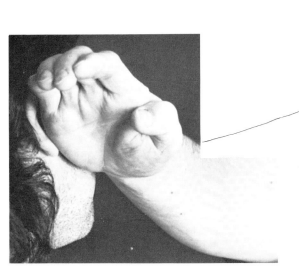

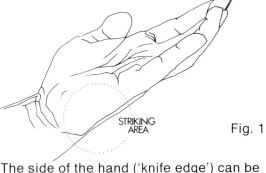

Fig. 1

The side of the hand ('knife edge') can be used in blocking and striking techniques. In this photograph the attacker's jaw hinge is being struck. Other target points to aim for are the temple, the collar bone and the throat.

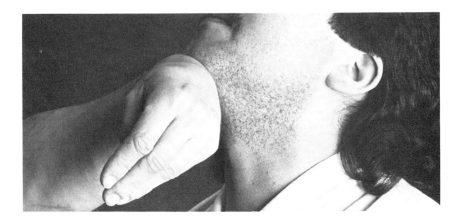

Fig. 2

The wrist can be used to strike the chin or nose. Notice that the fingers are held together and the thumb is tucked in. (If you push your fingers well back, your wrist will become quite prominent and tense. This will, in turn, make for a better, stronger technique.)

Fig. 3

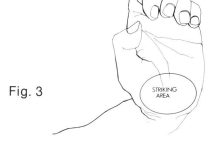

Front view of the palm heel, showing the muscular part of the hand used for striking and blocking.

Grabbing and pinching

To grab or pinch firmly can be extrememly painful to an opponent. The best areas to aim for are the insides of the legs and arms, and the groin. If an attacker has your head in a scissors hold between his legs you can pinch or grab (using a twisting motion) the inside of them to cause pain and to force him to release you.

Using the elbow

The elbow is particularly useful for striking at different angles and from different positions, and it is also very versatile as a block. If you have any physical disabilities with your hands, you can concentrate on using your elbow to defend yourself.

Make sure you fold your arm well back to make the elbow prominent. The elbow can strike forwards, sideways, backwards, or in an upward or downward motion, depending on the angle from which you are being attacked.

Side view of an elbow strike.

Using the head

The head is useful for close defensive measures. (I feel women and children should avoid using their heads if possible, because the wrong application could cause more problems than the one immediately presenting itself.) Aim with the centre of your skull projecting forwards. If you are grabbed from behind, you could throw your head backwards to try to catch the attacker's nose.

Leg techniques
(front kick, side kick, back kick, stamping kick)

Leg techniques can be very strong and effective, and they have the added advantage of enabling victims to keep a certain amount of distance between themselves and the attackers. However, they are usually much slower to perform than, for example, a hand technique. Although a well trained martial arts practitioner who specialises in leg techniques may be quick, most people find that hand techniques are generally faster to execute.

Using the knee
The knee is especially useful if you find your attacker is in close proximity to you, e.g. he has grabbed you, bear-hugged you or pinned you against a wall. A knee can be brought up between the attacker's legs to strike at the groin.

A knee strike to the face. The attacker's ears have been grabbed and his head has been pulled down to meet the victim's knee!

Using the heel

Whether you have shoes on or not, the heel can be a strong force when striking your attacker, especially if he is on the ground (use a stamping kick). More advanced students use the heel when executing back kicking techniques to rear attacks and they can aim as high as the face, depending upon their suppleness. However, this is not always necessary, as a good strike to the shin can be extremely painful and it is easy for most people to do. If you are wearing shoes with heels a strike down the aggressor's shin is most unpleasant!

A heel strike to the groin area from a rear attack.

Ball of the foot

Kick forwards at the attacker's groin, solar plexus, shin or kidneys with the ball of your foot and bend your toes as far back as possible to prevent them being broken during the kick. If you are wearing shoes the latter precaution is not too crucial, as long as your shoes give *good* protection to your toes. (You may not be able to bend your toes back in some footwear, but if you are wearing soft slippers, which give you no protection, it is important still to bend your toes back to avoid injury.)

Being on the floor, the victim is in a very vulnerable position. However, he can use this to his advantage by executing a strong kicking technique to the attacker's groin area. This will incapacitate the attacker whilst allowing the victim to keep his distance from him.

Top of the foot

The top part of the foot can be used to strike the groin area. Push the toes downwards when executing this technique to tense the foot and so enhance a strong technique.

A front kick to the groin using the top part of the foot.

Side of the foot

If an attacker grabs your arm or wrist from the side, you can use the side of your foot to strike his shin, knee, groin or even high up the body, i.e. solar plexus, depending on how supple you are.

Posture

When applying self-defence techniques always try to have a good upright posture. Leaning either forwards or backwards, or from side to side, means loss of body power and you could find yourself losing balance very easily and perhaps even falling over with your aggressor when trying to execute a technique. There are basic stances you can practise and if you consider looking into martial arts you will discover there are a variety of stances that can be adapted for different situations and techniques. However, in this book I will keep everything as basic and as straightforward as possible. The important point to remember is to keep your feet approximately shoulder width apart so that your weight is evenly distributed and you have a good foundation (see photograph on next page). Note that the man to the right of the picture has an incorrect stance and posture.

The man on the left has a correct upright posture and good balance. The man on the right is awkwardly positioned, mainly because his feet are not shoulder-width apart and he is leaning backwards.

Scream (Kia)

'Kia' is a Japanese term describing the exhalation of air when executing a technique. Kia helps to combine mental and physical elements into one force, so an individual feels totally committed to using a technique without hesitation. In karate it tends to sound like a deep grunt, but there is no 'set' sound or noise. It is the result of a person combining the exhalation of air with a shout or scream, and has the added advantage of assisting the body to become tense and therefore stronger when performing a manoeuvre. In a street situation the use of a scream has the extra bonus of attracting attention, so it is important to make as much noise as possible. It can also be most unnerving for the aggressor. (Native tribes used screams and shouts *before* they went into battle to instil fear into the enemy!) To scream suddenly at an attacker could assist in deterring him from continuing with an assault.

Blocking techniques

Forearm

The forearm can be used in various positions to counter-attack or strike an aggressor. If you have an overhead attack coming towards you it is a natural reaction to put your arms up to protect yourself, so why not adapt this response into a strong, defensive

Blocking with the forearm against a grab.

blocking technique? In the photograph below the arm is at an angle so that the force of the blow will slide down the forearm, making it easier to execute an effective block, i.e. to ride the force. It is also advisable to step back simultaneously to minimise the attack. If your block is not as successful as you would have hoped for, it is possible the aggressor could still miss you because of your evasive action.

Blocking against a forward attack. The block should be made at arm's length so that the offensive weapon is kept well away from the head. Blocking too short or too close could result in the weapon still making contact .

A punch to the body can be parried by side-stepping and using the forearm to deflect the blow.

Various

Not only can you use your forearm to block an attack effectively, but you can also use open hand, elbow, knee and leg techniques (although the knee and leg blocking techniques are quite advanced).

Blocking a front kick with the forearm. Note that the defender has moved forty-five degrees away from the attacker, which enables him to make an effective block with minimal body contact.

Evasive manoeuvres

Blocking can be particularly useful when combined with side-stepping or other evasive action.

Side-stepping is important for skirting your attacker's force. If your block is not successful, or not as successful as you had hoped, by moving away, i.e. straight back either 45 degrees to the right or left, or forwards either 45 degrees to the right or left, there is a good chance the attacker will miss you and you will then be in an advantageous position for counter-attacking.

Blocking by moving 45 degrees forwards to the inside of the attacker.

Blocking with the knife hand and moving backwards away from the attack.

Pressure points

When in restricted situations, i.e. when the attacker is very close, has the advantage or is on top of the victim, it is difficult to execute or apply a 'hard' technique, such as a punch, with any force. However, you can create distance and move the aggressor away by applying pressure on certain nerve points which will cause pain. You will then be able to execute a 'hard' technique to immobilise him. This is a particularly advanced area of self defence and you should be supervised when learning the exact location of the nerve points and how to apply pressure correctly.

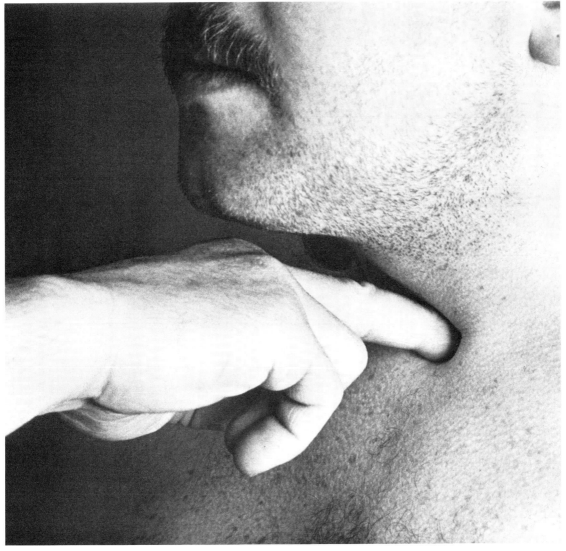

Finger strike to the throat which could cause considerable discomfort to an attacker.

Suggested striking techniques to vulnerable areas

Below is a list of striking techniques to vulnerable areas shown in figures 4 and 5 which can be employed when both parties are in a standing position. Although kicking techniques have been suggested for the lower part of the body, should the defender be small in stature compared with the aggressor, or should he be in a kneeling position, then elbow and fist techniques to the groin and lower regions would work well (remember that the aggressor will probably lose his balance after the victim's strike, so the latter should move quickly out of the way so that he doesn't fall on top of him).

Front view

1 Front punch; elbow
2 Inverted back fist; hammer fist; elbow; knife edge of hand
3 Fingers; knuckles
4 Front fist; hammer fist; inverted back fist; elbow; palm heel; knife edge of hand; knee (when pulling the head downwards)
5 Elbow; knife edge of hand; hammer fist; back knuckle fist
6 Front fist; elbow; palm heel
7 Roundhouse fist; elbow; back knuckle fist
8 Front punch; elbow
9 Front punch; knuckle (ridge hand); knife edge; spear hand (finger thrust)
10 Knife edge; elbow; hammer fist
11 Circular disengagement wrist techniques
12 Front punch; elbow; front, back or side kick if legs are flexible
13 Knife edge block or bite
14 Front punch; elbow; front, back or side kick

15 Front kick; knee; hammer fist from rear; ridge hand; grab; rear kick (heel) to rear attack; front punch; knife edge of hand
16 Thumb lever; back knuckle fist; elbow strike to make opponent release grab
17 Hand lever and as for 16
18 Finger lever and as for 16
19 Kicking techniques, e.g. knife edge of foot
20 Kicking techniques, e.g. knife edge of foot
21 Heel (stamping kick)

Back view

1 Finger or thumb to pressure point (must be accurate on exact point)
2 Front punch; elbow; kick
3 Elbow
4 Front punch; elbow; kick
5 Leg techniques – side kick using knife edge of foot or ball of foot
6 Same as for 5

Remember that with the execution of certain techniques on very vulnerable areas the results can be quite severe, so never play around practising vigorously on friends – it is extremely dangerous. Restrict the use of self-defence techniques only to when it is absolutely necessary.

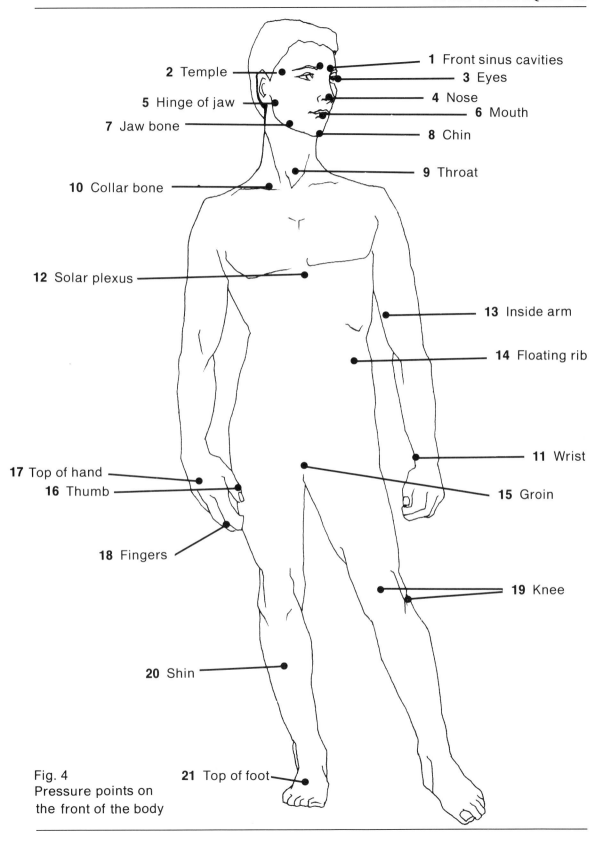

1 Front sinus cavities
2 Temple
3 Eyes
5 Hinge of jaw
4 Nose
6 Mouth
7 Jaw bone
8 Chin
9 Throat
10 Collar bone
12 Solar plexus
13 Inside arm
14 Floating rib
11 Wrist
17 Top of hand
16 Thumb
15 Groin
18 Fingers
19 Knee
20 Shin
21 Top of foot

Fig. 4
Pressure points on
the front of the body

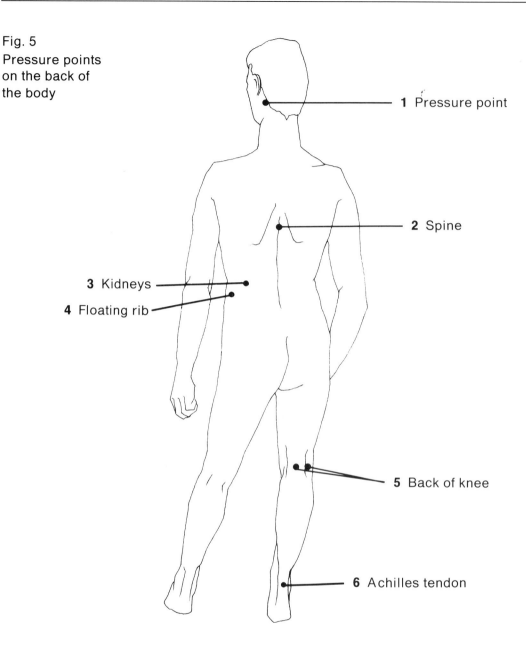

Fig. 5
Pressure points
on the back of
the body

1 Pressure point

2 Spine

3 Kidneys

4 Floating rib

5 Back of knee

6 Achilles tendon

I have only touched on elementary self-defence principles, but further on in the book you will see that these basic techniques can be used very effectively in various everyday situations.

I have tried to cover as many predictable circumstances as possible, although no two situations or attacks are the same and it is impossible to generalise about a 'typical' attacker. An attacker can be anyone from a rather inoffensive, small, slim person to a tall, heavy, arrogant individual, so the motto is 'Be prepared' for anyone or anything.

2
DEFENCE AGAINST OUTDOOR ATTACKS

There are many situations in which you could be attacked. I have chosen to describe and illustrate a varied selection of locations, attacks and counter-attacks to show how different self-defence techniques can be applied successfully.

Woodland area

Side attack

Take a situation in which a woman is walking home down a country lane or park area and is suddenly grabbed from the side. Her mental approach should be one of determination not to let the attacker succeed in his intentions and she should 'switch on' to becoming aggressive herself. This alone can be a deterrent. Attackers do not normally expect their victims suddenly to look aggressive and to retaliate. The use of 'kia' (the scream when exhaling air, which helps the mind and body co-ordinate) would also be very effective here.

The first and most important rule always is to aim counter-attacks at the opponent's vulnerable areas: do not waste time and energy throwing everything into a hard (muscle) area, e.g. chest, top of arms, which will have no effect whatsoever. It does not matter how tall or heavy the attacker is, since everyone has the same vulnerable parts of the body. These are not always protected, especially the face—which is why I particularly recommend the majority of defensive strikes to be made to this area. There are other vulnerable areas if you should happen to miss the initial target, i.e. you may strike the attacker in the eye, mouth or chin instead of the nose. The important factor is that you have made contact and, hopefully, incapacitated the assailant.

Often the attacker's body will be well protected by clothing, e.g. he may be wearing a heavy leather jacket or coat, but it is very rare that the face will be covered unless he is wearing, for example, a motorbike helmet! In the latter case you would concentrate your strikes lower down the body. The assailant would have the added disadvantage of lack of manoeuvrability in the helmet and his vision would be slightly impaired, making his reactions slower than normal. These points could all be utilised to your advantage.

In the following reconstruction of an attack the victim will use one of the basic techniques described on pages 10 and 15.

The attacker has made his initial grab from behind the tree where he was hiding (photograph 1). The victim punches the attacker in the face with a good tight fist. She has caught him on the point of the chin (photograph 2). There are a lot of vulnerable areas on the face, which is why it is a good area to aim for; also, it is very

The attacker makes his initial grab to the victim's right side.

The victim punches out immediately, aiming for the attacker's face region. She hits the point of his chin, but just as effective targets here would have been his nose or eyes.

rarely covered with clothing that can afford some protection. With the face being fully exposed, she could hit him on the nose, in the eye, on the temple, or on the jaw.

A good strong punch on the point of the chin, even by a woman or child, can render an attacker unconscious or at least will imbalance him slightly, giving the victim a chance to do a follow-up technique.

It does not matter whether you use your right or left fist. It depends totally on the situation and how you are seized. In this case the right arm has been caught so it is more practical and effective to use the left fist. Alternatively, if the attacker had come from the left side of the victim, grabbing her left arm, then the right fist would have been more appropriate.

It is important, therefore, to develop both hands effectively to strike a blow. The same applies to leg techniques. Avoid practising just one side, e.g. only your right fist. Make as many parts of your body as possible into effective weapons so that in the event of, for instance, an injury incapacitating one of your limbs you could still cope well in a dangerous attack situation. For example, if you had broken your right arm and you were attacked you would have to rely on your left fist or leg techniques.

Without hesitation, the victim takes hold of the attacker's hair and pulls his head down onto her knee. A severe blow could cause an injured nose and eye watering, and would allow the victim time to run away.

3

The impact of the victim's knee coming up to meet the attacker's face should be enough to incapacitate him for some time, especially if it catches his nose region!

In photograph 3 the defender has followed through the defence by seizing the attacker's hair. This particular attacker has plenty of hair, but if you are attacked by a bald aggressor simply grab the back of his head or his ears! Pull the head downwards while simultaneously bringing your knee up for immediate impact (see photograph 4). A good knee strike into the aggressor's face should catch his nose and, depending upon the severity of the technique, the aggressor could receive a broken nose and other complicated injuries, such as breakage of the sinus bone, heavy bleeding, watering eyes, impaired vision, etc. This, of course, would render the aggressor helpless and would give you a chance to get away!

Once you have disarmed or restrained the attacker it is important to get someone to contact the police immediately or do so yourself if there is no one around. Also, ask for an ambulance if you feel you have done severe damage to the aggressor. Do not stop and think, 'What shall I do now?', for it may give the assailant time to get away. Remember, he may strike again and the next victim may not be so lucky.

It is easy to be wise after the event, but try to remember the following principles:

1   Turn your fear and surprise into aggression and channel this towards striking the assailant.

2   Make sure he will not get back up and continue the assault.

3   Make sure he is restrained either by yourself or by other people while the police are called.

4   When in a difficult situation, calm yourself both mentally and physically by taking relaxed, deep breaths.

Street defence

Attack from the rear

Street attacks are commonplace and, again, victims range from very young children and mothers with children to old age pensioners.

In the next sequence a teenager is out shopping. She is totally involved in what she is doing and the last thing she expects is to be attacked outside the supermarket. Attacks happen very quickly and sometimes other people will not become involved because they think it is possibly a domestic problem or because they are frightened. If you ever see anything suspicious happening in the street do not hesitate: call the police, give them the details and they can decide whether or not to investigate further. All too often people hesitate, do nothing, and a crime is committed against an innocent party. Crime is on the increase and criminals are more blatant than ever because the public do not always respond or bother to take notice. Put yourself in the victim's place and your reaction may be quite different!

In the reconstruction the attack occurs in broad daylight near a shopping centre. The prospective attacker is relying on his quick action to get money or even to abduct the victim into a nearby car. If he intends to take the money, he will probably run off into the shops or crowds in the hope it will be difficult to catch him. If his intention is to abduct the victim, he could try to make out it is a domestic disagreement; people do not like interfering when they think the couple know each other and the matter is personal. This particular attack could happen anywhere to anyone, day or night, with or without people in the vicinity.

The victim is preoccupied with placing her shopping into the boot of her car and is unaware of the prospective attacker behind her.

A vicious grab to the victim's hair.

Whatever the reason for the attack, we shall assume the victim is placing her shopping into the boot of her car and she is grabbed from behind by the attacker (see photographs 1 and 2). The attacker is very close behind, so the ideal counter-attack is to swing round with the elbow aiming directly at the attacker's face (see photograph 3).

This elbow technique is very effective for warding off a rear attack.

To make sure she has caught him she turns round fully and follows up with a second elbow attack to the face, aiming under the

chin (see photograph 4). (*Note*: photograph 3 shows the use of a side roundhouse elbow technique, while photograph 4 shows the use of the elbow in an upward motion. Both are very effective, strong techniques aimed at the attacker's vulnerable areas. The term 'roundhouse' is applied to any technique in which the striking part of the body travels in an arc, rather than in a straight line.) She pushes the attacker away and calls for assistance. There are, of course, a number of further follow-up techniques she could use from this position, e.g. knee to the groin, selection of punches or kicks.

To make sure the attacker does not persist with the assault, the victim follows through with an uppercut elbow strike.

Gully or passage way

Knife attack from the left side

The next attack takes place, once again, during the day. The attacker has a knife, which makes the situation most dangerous. It is bad enough to be attacked at all, but when a weapon of any description is used, such as a knife, broken bottle, wooden club or metal bar, the predicament is far more serious.

Ideally, in these circumstances you should keep your distance as much as possible and, if the attacker is intent on using the weapon, you have nothing to lose in doing your utmost to defend yourself straight away. In the reconstruction the victim will have no time to talk her way out of the situation, because she has been taken completely by surprise and has to act *immediately*. Notice she is wearing a pencil skirt and high heel shoes which will make it difficult for her to run (although if the opportunity presents itself you should always *run*!)

The attacker lunges forwards from behind the wall with the knife (see photograph 1). The victim steps back to keep a safe

The attack is coming from the victim's left side. This time she has the additional horror of having to contend with the attacker's knife.

distance from the knife and blocks with the side of her hand (photograph 2). Notice her body is at an angle to the attacker so that she presents a small target to him. It is important to keep your guard up in front of your body for protection and do not be afraid to block or parry the arm holding the knife with your hands or arms. It is far better to take a cut or graze in the hands or arms than to receive a serious or fatal wound in the body's vital organs. Although unpleasant, your hands and arms will recover! Try not to hesitate when a weapon is coming towards you. Use evasive action by stepping back or to the side and simultaneously apply the block. The main objective is to avoid any contact with the knife.

Many people have survived knife attacks to the body by unintentionally having an arm in the way, so if you were to make this into an effective blocking technique you might receive no injury at all.

This photograph shows the importance of using a block with a forty-five degree body movement.

After a successful block, and to prevent the attacker wielding the knife again, the victim takes hold of his wrist and keeps the knife at arm's length. She counter-attacks with a kick to the man's groin.

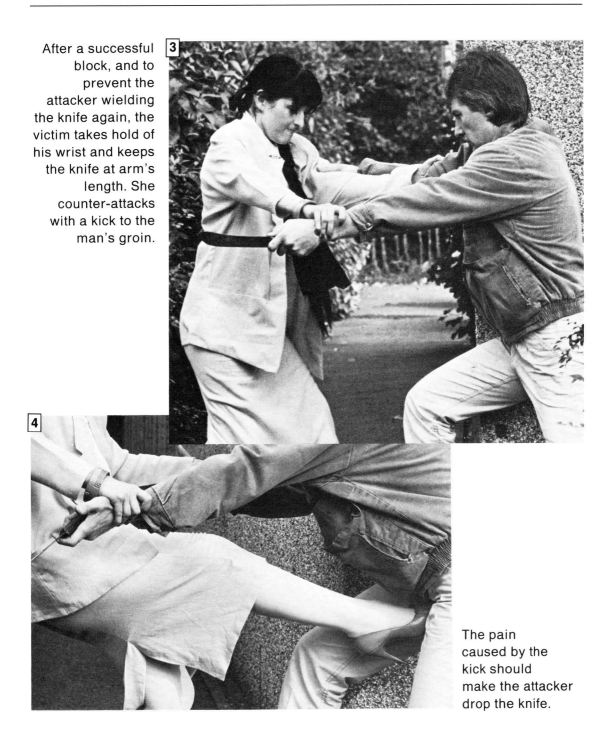

The pain caused by the kick should make the attacker drop the knife.

After executing the block and keeping the knife at bay (see photograph 3), the victim kicks the attacker in the groin area (photograph 4) (her feet are protected by her shoes, but if a shoe had fallen off she would have used the top part of her foot to prevent injury to her toes).

If the knife were not released, the victim could use an upward knee strike to the attacker's elbow joint, simultaneously turning his palm upwards. Ideally, this technique needs to strike just above the elbow joint and may result in temporary paralysis of the arm.

Note the height from which the victim executes an elbow strike for maximum power and effect. She aims between the attacker's shoulder blades, directly onto his vertebrae. This type of strike is extremely dangerous and should be used only when absolutely essential: it can result in fracturing of vertebrae (causing partial paralysis), dizziness and difficulty in breathing.

She seizes the attacker's shoulder/arm with her left hand and draws her knee up towards his elbow joint, simultaneously pushing the attacker's arm downwards (photograph 5). This will cause severe pain and will make the attacker drop the knife. Coupled with the pain from the kicking technique to the groin, he has bent over. This has lined him up for a finishing technique of an elbow into the back. For maximum impact it is important to start this technique as high as possible (see photographs 6 and 7). The victim forces her elbow between the assailant's shoulder blades, she grabs the knife and *runs!* She calls for help and telephones the police.

The final elbow strike hits the target area.

Note: once the knife or any weapon is out of an attacker's hand, immediately follow through with an immobilising technique. Do not allow him to retrieve the weapon.

Self defence at night

Although broad daylight attacks are becoming commoner, even in busy streets, night attacks are a major area of concern. The attacker feels safer at night because it is, of course, more difficult for the victim to see the aggressor's face. The assailant can also conceal himself much better at night before making his attack, i.e. in a shop doorway or alleyway, or by a wall, etc. So, it is very important not to walk too close to these 'risk areas'. Also, try to walk towards the edge of the pavement, which enables you to see better into door-ways and reduces the chance of a sudden grab. Even though I practise martial arts and have done so for many years, I would not be so foolish as to tempt fate and take unnecessary risks – no one is *invincible!* Avoid walking home alone if at all possible: go home with friends, take a taxi or arrange for a lift with someone you know and trust; even if it costs you a little extra to get home, it is money well spent.

Caution should be used in security at home, too. Make sure you have good locks and do not open your door or let anyone in until you are sure you know them and it is safe to do so. If you are unsure about your home security, contact your local police who will make arrangements to come out and give you the necessary advice on your particular property. Remember that some insur-ance policies are void if your locks are poor or non-existent.

When all precautions have been taken there may still be the odd occasion when you could be in a dangerous situation through no fault of your own. Attacks have been known to take place when a victim has just popped next door to see a neighbour for a few minutes.

A major disadvantage of a night attack is that your vision is obviously impaired, but this also applies to the attacker! You have, therefore, to rely more on your senses of hearing and smell and on general awareness, which are enhanced with loss of vision. (Blind people have a tremendous hearing ability and awareness of things around them.)

If you are attacked in the dark, it is usually preferable to hold onto the attacker so you can get some idea about his size and position. This will enable you to aim your counter-attack to a vulnerable area more accurately.

3
DEFENCE AGAINST INDOOR ATTACKS

Wine bar

Defence from a sitting position (chair technique)

People are not always attacked from a standing position and in the next reconstruction the victim will be attacked while seated in a chair.

The intended victim is enjoying an evening with either family or friends in a local wine bar/hotel/public house. They are in a relaxed mood and the prospective aggressor could be anyone from a person who has had too much to drink, or who does not know the group and has unfortunately picked on an individual, to someone who knows the people and has a personal grievance. The aggressor attempts to grab the victim around the throat and to pull her out of the chair.

This particular aggressor has had too much to drink and has been 'eyeing up' the prospective victim. He tries a verbal approach but she politely rebuffs him. He does not take 'No' for an answer and under the influence of the drink he decides to make a grab for her. He seizes her around the throat, with the intention of pulling her up and out of the chair. (Remember, some people are greatly affected by drink and act totally out of character, e.g. become a general nuisance, argumentative, aggressive or violent, when usually they are very placid by nature.)

With all throat holds try to tense your throat while executing a self-defence technique to relieve the pressure and to enable you to continue breathing! In this particular instance the victim has brought her one hand up to pull the aggressor's arm down to assist in relieving the pressure around her throat. She simultaneously strikes with her other fist into the aggressor's face (photograph 1).

In this rather unexpected situation, a drunk aggressor takes hold of a woman by her throat. She retaliates with an upward punch straight into his nose.

While the attacker is concentrating on his nose injury, the victim applies a thumb lever to take him down to the floor.

Even though you may be unable to see the aggressor's face if he is attacking from behind, you can usually sense his presence and whereabouts by his breathing, by his voice if he talks to you, or, as in this case, by the odour of drink!

Even a slight tap will cause pain, discomfort and even a nose bleed. So, as the aggressor holds on to his nose, the victim seizes the opportunity to make him release his grip by applying a thumb lock (photograph 2). This is simply a matter of pulling the thumb away from the fingers.

She then proceeds to take him down onto the floor (photograph 3). (Do not *throw* an aggressor down, as you could find yourself going with him! Instead, as you apply the thumb lock, imagine you are bringing your hand down towards your own legs. This will also keep the thumb lock on securely.)

From there, the security officer has come to the rescue and he proceeds to throw the culprit out or call the police, depending on the severity of the situation.

Place of work

Gun attacks

Banks are now usually well equipped with alarm bells and video cameras, but there are still small corner shops, post offices, etc. which do not possess such equipment and it is not unusual for attackers on these premises to carry guns.

In a gun attack situation, *do nothing*!

It is very rare for anyone to apply or execute a technique successfully against someone with a gun; it is so easy and quick for the trigger to be pulled, although this may not have been the initial intention of the attacker. A gun is usually used as a threat to get what is wanted and it is not often that it will actually be fired (although you should always be aware of the possibility). The best form of self defence is to try to keep calm and quiet. Move slowly and do exactly as you are instructed. The gunman will probably be very nervous and any sudden movement may make him more jumpy and likely to pull the trigger without thinking.

If you do get the opportunity to talk, be polite – the wrong attitude and action could incite the gunman to use the weapon.

Try to remember as much as you can about the attacker: his appearance, voice, movements, anything out of the ordinary which will help the police to catch him. This will also give you something to think about and help you to keep calm.

Deep breathing will be helpful, too. Inhale through the nose and down into the pit of the stomach, hold for a few seconds and exhale slowly through the mouth.

When the gunman has gone and you feel it is safe, call the police immediately.

Use of restraining techniques

There are a number of different work environments which carry a high risk factor. However, if you cause injury during the course of your duty/employment to a patient, pupil, parent, employee, employer, customer, etc. you could find yourself in a lot of trouble, not only from your employers but also legally. The individual concerned could take legal action against *you* and it is then up to you to prove your case as self defence. Therefore, it is far better to try to use restraining techniques in this sort of environment so that you can defend yourself without harm to your aggressor. Such techniques are the most preferable form of self defence, especially when you are dealing with a friend, relative or someone who does not intend to harm you but perhaps has had too much to drink, is out of control, is emotionally upset or is mentally or physically ill. The last thing you want to do is cause physical injury to this person and you must also try to prevent him causing any injury to himself.

The risk of attack, therefore, can vary greatly, depending on the work environment. People in high risks areas include police, shopkeepers, nurses and teachers, to name but a few. I have taken an example from just one high risk area: the participant in the following sequence is a school teacher by profession and a similar incident to that portrayed actually happened to her.

The teacher is experiencing unrest in the class and it is highlighted by one pupil who starts to show off and generally take advantage of the situation. He becomes verbally aggressive and makes it difficult for the teacher to leave the classroom to get help.

As the pupil makes a grab for the teacher she immediately disengages the wrist, executes a wrist lock and takes him down onto the desk. She keeps him pinned down by applying her body weight to the wrist lock. There is no physical injury whatsoever, but the more the pupil struggles the more painful it becomes for him.

A wrist disengagement is applied by using the principle of the circle to break the opponent's grip. It does not require strength, just pure technique. To struggle against force by using force means you could find yourself there all day and no one will move. So, the answer is to harmonise by accepting the force and then to re-direct it back towards the aggressor. You are therefore using his own force against him, with very little effort from you. This works extremely well against a number of grabbing attacks and, remember, no strength is needed.

The teacher then makes a firm stand while still keeping the pupil in the wrist lock and instructs one of the other students to fetch the headteacher and explain the situation. Now that the 'leader' is 'out of action', this should deter any other children, who may have been supporting him, to intervene.

The teacher is in control and should tell the rest of the class to behave and sit quietly. Once they see she can take care of herself and she will stand no nonsense they should do as she orders.

It is important to be positive in such instances and not to show any weakness. *Do not show fear.* Usually these sort of attackers are bullies and cowards at heart and if you show fear they will thrive on it, but if you reflect calmness and are positive in the way you talk and act this in itself can be a deterrent. You may be shaking inside but try not to let them see or know that you are!

Alternative defence (1)

The pupil could have taken hold of the teacher's arm instead of her wrist. In this situation, the following techniques could have been applied.

The pupil grabs the teacher's arm and proceeds to punch her with his left fist in the face. The teacher blocks the fist using the knife edge block (photograph 1). (You should never feel restricted to using just this technique; see the variations in chapter 1 and try adapting these blocks to the same attack. The most important factor is to stop the attack!)

She then uses a circular movement to disengage the grip, simultaneously moving in close to apply the arm lock. Note that she grabs the pupil's arm at the elbow joint at the same time as twisting her left wrist and arm over the pupil's right arm.

From here she pushes the boy down onto the desk, applying the lock to the arm as in the first defence, and leans her body weight well over the pupil, keeping him firmly in place until help arrives. The more the pupil struggles to get free, the more painful it should be for him as the lock is kept in place (see photographs 2, 3 and 4).

The important point here is that the pupil has been restrained without injury, other than perhaps hurting his pride in front of his classmates.

The teacher demonstrates the effectiveness of the knife hand block.

The arm lever is effective in this situation for restraining the pupil without injury.

The teacher places her right hand on the back of the pupil's neck and brings her left arm up towards her throat.

Keeping her bodyweight well over the pupil, the teacher restrains him by keeping his left arm secure and by applying her weight as pressure.

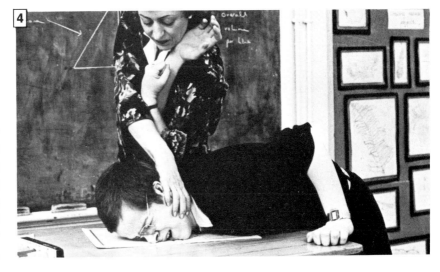

Alternative defence (2)

This time the pupil has already taken hold of the teacher with his left hand and is moving in to grab with the right (photograph 1).

As the pupil is not punching but is making a grab it is not so important to block in this particular instance. The teacher goes straight for a throat hold before his right hand has got hold of her (photograph 2).(*Note*: there are various pressure points in the throat and with this particular grab you can successfully restrain an aggressor by applying pressure to nerve points without causing any physical damage or injury.)

The teacher then reverses the hold the pupil has on her with his left hand by seizing his left arm and pinning him up against the blackboard (photograph 3). (*Note*: she has kept her body to one side and not directly in front of him. There are more advanced techniques where you can use your body weight to pin and restrain the aggressor, but in this particular instance it is best for the teacher to keep her body to the side of the pupil to prevent him 'kneeing' or kicking her – which would be easy to do if she stood directly in front of him. It is important to keep the throat lock on: the more he struggles, the more discomfort he will inflict upon himself.)

The pupil seizes the teacher.

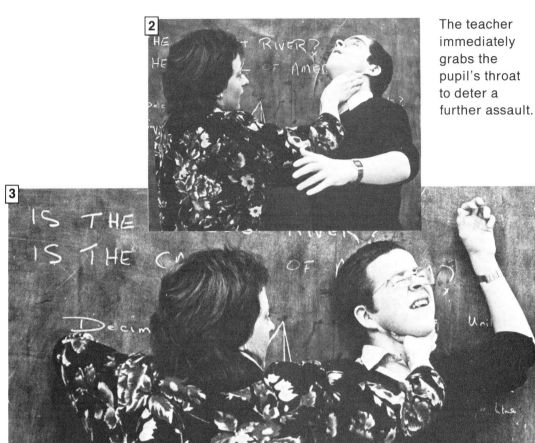

The teacher immediately grabs the pupil's throat to deter a further assault.

Three variations of restraining techniques have now been demonstrated and have worked successfully without anyone coming to physical harm. What is more, the risk factor of the teacher having legal action taken against her or of her being in serious trouble with her employers is no longer a great threat because she has defended herself without injury to either party. (*Note*: the Education Authorities have special guidelines for staff, but if teachers cannot get help or cannot prevent an attack they are, by law, entitled to defend themselves by using reasonable restraint (as mentioned in chapter 10).)

I must stress again here that physical contact should always be avoided if there is a feasible alternative, especially in a work environment. The school examples in this chapter are not to be treated as isolated cases. They have been included to represent many diverse places of work where employees can be at risk, through no fault of their own, in carrying out their duties.

The teacher continues with the throat grasp until the pupil is pinned against the wall. No harm is inflicted, except that the more the pupil struggles, the more pain and discomfort he will bring upon himself.

4

SELF DEFENCE
FOR CHILDREN

At school

All parents worry about their children's safety, but if a child obeys the instructions given by parents, guardians and teachers he should usually be safe. Safety points are listed below. Children should:

1   Never go anywhere with a stranger or strangers.

2   Never get into a car or any vehicle with a stranger or strangers.

3   Never accept sweets or gifts from a stranger or strangers.

4   Never play or go anywhere out of sight, especially on their own.

5   Never play outside after dark.

6   Always tell their parents, guardian or teacher where they are going and if they change those arrangements let them know! They should never wander off alone without telling anybody.

7   Always go home with a friend(s) and never take short cuts which are lonely, no matter how much time they will save.

8   Always tell their parents, guardian or teacher if someone approaches them in a suspicious manner.

Advice for parents/guardians/teachers

1 If possible always take children to a destination and collect them. Avoid letting them go anywhere on their own or with people you do not know or you know very little about.

2 Do not let young children go to the shops on their own, no matter how close and especially when it is starting to get dark. Children like to go shopping on their own, but if you can accompany them, or at least watch them go down the road into the shop and back home again, it is far safer. The fatal mistake often made is thinking that because it is 'just down the road' or '5 minutes away' the child will be safe. It can take less than a minute to abduct a child, so *be careful*!

3 Make sure your child is completely aware of potential dangers and understands all the points mentioned above.

Unfortunately, even if all the above rules have been remembered there may still be the unforeseen occasion when an attacker will catch a child off guard.

In the next set of pictures, a 7-year-old girl is coming home from school. The attacker looks innocent enough and calls to the child, asking a typical question which will attract her attention. Without thinking, the child goes over; she is just outside the school gates, looking for her mother who is late, and she still feels she is 'safe'. The attacker could have been observing this particular child for some days and noticed that the mother always arrives late to collect her. His car is close by and he has an excuse to use if the mother should arrive and catch him in the process, i.e. he is waiting for his own child and thought he could help. The child has already been well cautioned by her mother and teacher about strangers and is reluctant to go with him. She reacts accordingly.

The child innocently comes out of the school gates and the attacker makes a grab for her (photograph 1). Even though he is

The attacker attempts to seize the child after she refuses to go with him willingly.

twice her size she makes maximum use of her body weight and throws her school bag, which contains books, into his groin (photograph 2). If she did not have a bag or the bag was only light, she could have used her leg to kick him in the shin region, just below the knee, or to the groin if she could comfortably reach that target (this would all depend on the height of the child in relation to the aggressor, i.e. tall child, small aggressor).

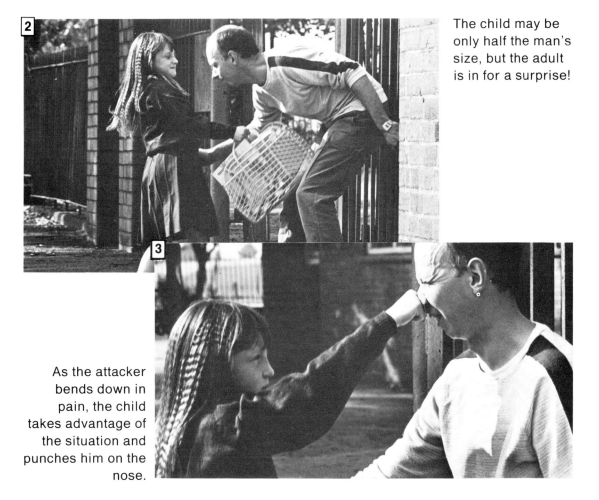

The child may be only half the man's size, but the adult is in for a surprise!

As the attacker bends down in pain, the child takes advantage of the situation and punches him on the nose.

The girl may only have stunned the man but as he bends down with discomfort she immediately punches him on the nose (photograph 3). He has come down to her height so she uses this to her advantage! The fact that the child has retaliated should attract attention from other people in the vicinity, who should come to the child's aid.

This will give her time to run back into the school and to security. Teachers should be informed immediately and the incident should be reported to the police.

Enticement into a car

Using kicking techniques

Another good self-defence technique, especially for children, is leg kicking. It allows a child to keep some distance between him and the abductor. The added advantage of using leg techniques is that children's legs are usually fairly strong. The main objective, because of the probable difference in height, is to aim low. This is easy for a child to do and can still cause great discomfort to the adult.

A car pulls over by a 9-year-old boy (photograph 1). Notice there is a couple in the car. Children sometimes feel safe when they see two people, because they associate this with their own parents and they believe it is only dangerous if *one* person approaches, usually a man. Children should be warned *not to approach strangers generally*.

The car occupants could ask numerous questions: anything, they think, that would entice the child willingly into the car and would not attract attention or suspicion from passers-by. Examples could be:

(a) 'Would you like to go for a ride?'

(b) 'We are friends of your mother and she has asked us to pick you up.'

(c) 'Your mother/father has been taken ill and we/I have been sent to pick you up.'

(d) 'Would you like some sweets?'

A young boy thinks he is being helpful by giving directions, but he is unaware that the occupiers of the car have malevolent intentions.

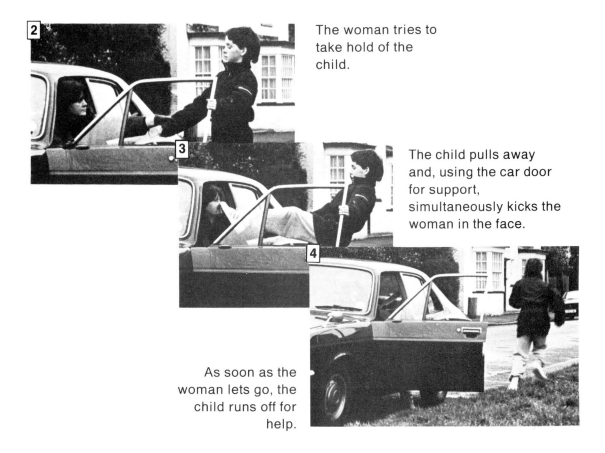

2 The woman tries to take hold of the child.

3 The child pulls away and, using the car door for support, simultaneously kicks the woman in the face.

4 As soon as the woman lets go, the child runs off for help.

The passenger, who is a woman, has already opened the car door to speak to the child. As the child declines the offer she makes a sudden lunge to pull him into the car (photograph 2).

The child tries to pull away but is unable to break the grip. As the adult is sitting down, the child uses this to his advantage to keep his distance and kicks the woman in the face, aiming for the nose (photograph 3).

The woman releases immediately due to extreme pain and this gives the child a chance to run off (see photograph 4). (Note: in these circumstances children should *not linger*. They should go straight home immediately and inform their parents, who should, in turn, notify the police. If they are a long way from home, they could knock on someone's door and ask them to call their parents or the police, or they could dial '999' themselves and inform the police of the incident. They should try to remember as much as they can about the occupants of the car, i.e. their age, hair colour, regional accent, distinguishing marks, and about the car itself, i.e. its colour, make, registration or anything unusual about the vehicle. This will be very helpful to the police in trying to catch the attackers or at least in putting out a general warning to the public.)

Park area

All children love parks, with the swings and slides, but they are, unfortunately, very high risk areas if parents leave their children unattended. Prospective attackers can observe, usually without being noticed, and can then make an approach.

Here we have a 9-year-old boy playing with his friend at a local park, unaware he is being watched by a prospective attacker who is casually sitting on a nearby bench.

The attacker realises the child is not accompanied by an adult and therefore feels he is 'easy prey'.

The attacker calls to the boy in a friendly manner and tries to entice the child to go voluntarily with him by asking questions, such as:

(a) 'Would you like some sweets—there is a shop just over the road?'

(b) 'I have a lovely new car. Would you like to come for a ride? It would only take a few minutes!'

The child senses danger and politely refuses to go with the attacker and starts to walk away, back to his friend.

At this point the attacker, failing to entice the child to come along willingly, decides to make a grab for the boy with the intention of carrying him off either to his car or to a woodland area (photograph 1). Every child should avoid being picked up off the ground, if at all possible, as it places them in a very vulnerable position from which it is extremely difficult to apply a self-defence technique.

A child is being threatened by an adult. The boy aims for vulnerable areas below the man's waste, in this case his knee caps.

Note that the child uses the side of his left foot to avoid any injuries to his toes and he keeps his leg straight on impact for maximum effect.

To make sure the attacker will not pursue the assault, the child follows through with a right kick to the groin area.

As soon as the attacker has made his grab the child immediately kicks back and strikes the attacker's shin (photograph 2).

He then follows through with a further kick to the groin area with his right leg to incapacitate the attacker and to give himself time to get away (photograph 3).

Of course, a number of different techniques could be used in such a situation and it would not matter which leg was used for which technique. It would depend entirely upon which was the most natural for the child to use and which could cause the most damage to the attacker, according to his position of attack.

5

SELF DEFENCE FOR SENIOR CITIZENS

Senior citizens may feel that they are completely defenceless and vulnerable against attacks. However, it is quite possible for them to defend themselves successfully, according to their physical fitness, with the correct approach. This has been proven time and time again by elderly victims who have managed to ward off an attacker with sheer anger and totally unexpected fighting spirit.

Most prospective attackers, when approaching an elderly person, do not anticipate any resistance whatsoever, especially as in most cases it is often better to be agreeable and to let the attacker take the purse or whatever it is he is after than to receive physical injury. However, unfortunately, there have been, and still are, many reports of elderly people being attacked needlessly for valuables and being left with terrible injuries which, because of an invalidity, such as partial blindness, arthritis, being confined to a wheelchair, etc., they did not try to prevent. In this sort of situation the victim has no alternative but to attempt to defend himself in the best possible way. Not all senior citizens will be able to apply physical defence, but it is surprising how many dismiss the idea when they are more than capable of using self-defence techniques.

So, let's look at ways in which you can make the most of your body by using the most advantageous techniques and adapting them to your own individual ability. People suffering from arthritis may find it difficult to make a fist, so the fingers could be used to strike the attacker effectively in the eye area. Elbow techniques are also ideal for elderly people and are very strong in application. If a person's legs are his strongest asset, then leg techniques can be used. A senior citizen may not be able to kick very high, but a good, unexpected kick to the shin is most effective, especially when followed up with a face technique, and will give the victim time to get away from the attacker and call for help.

Attacks in the home

As already mentioned, people are not always attacked out of doors; it can be while they feel safe in the comfort of their own home. (See also the next chapter.) There is, of course, the situation in which an intruder, such as a burglar, enters a house during the day or night.

Initially, if this happens to you it is better not to approach an intruder on your own. Your life is more important than material objects, however angry you may feel about someone forcing his way into your property, and this applies to people of all ages. If at all possible, call the police immediately; preferably leave the house and call from a neighbour's home. If it is at night and you have an upstairs telephone extension, call from your bedroom and make sure, if you have a lock on the bedroom door, you lock the door first. If you do not have a telephone and it is difficult to leave the house unnoticed, open a window, shout for help and make as much noise as you possibly can to attract attention. You may find the police will come out on a 'Disturbance of the peace' call! Nevertheless, at least they will be on their way to help you, which is the prime objective.

If you are about to go into your house and you sense it has been broken into and that the burglar could still be present, *do not enter*; again, call the police immediately.

You may find yourself in the unfortunate position of not being able to do any of the above. The attacker could have the initial advantage if he has seen you first and you could be totally unaware of his presence. The next sequence of events portrays this type of situation, with the attacker/burglar having the advantage in that (a) he has spotted the victim first, and (b) the victim is a retired gentleman with a weak leg who has to use a walking stick for assistance. Bearing all this in mind, the victim will 'have a go' and do his utmost to defend himself by making use of what he has, i.e. the walking stick, to maximum advantage.

An elderly gentleman uses his walking stick to strike the intruder's nose.

Defence from the right side

The victim is coming down the stairs either to investigate noise or to get a drink.

The burglar makes a lunge with his left hand to seize the victim's right wrist or arm.

The victim utilises his walking stick, supported by his left hand for maximum impact, to strike the attacker on the nose (see photograph 1).

The victim then follows through with a strike to the groin area, using the walking stick (photograph 2).

To make sure the intruder is sufficiently incapacitated, the man strikes a second time.

The attacker falls back in pain and the victim continues his defence by either (a) striking downwards with the stick to the groin area, or (b) thrusting downwards with the point of the stick, again to the groin area (photograph 3).

So, what initially appeared to be a disadvantageous situation for the victim with a walking stick actually turned out to be advantageous, because he could use his stick to defend himself. Also, since he did not use his hands in defence, he made no direct physical contact with the burglar and therefore reduced any possibility of inflicting an injury upon himself.

A final strike to the intruder's groin gives the elderly man time to get away and seek help. (This sort of strike should be used only when absolutely necessary.)

6
RAPE ATTACKS

Rape is a very serious offence and, should you be or have been raped, do seek professional counselling (check your legal position as outlined on pages 88–9). The act of rape not only applies to women but also to men, boys and children. The word 'rape' means that a sexual act has been committed on an individual without his or her consent.

Rape is a very distressing experience and sometimes the victim feels degraded to the point of not being able to mention the incident for fear of ridicule. However, there is always very good professional help available to advise, comfort and support the victim. Counsellors will also try to help the victim overcome the trauma or at least come to terms with the situation and take the correct course of action. It is vital that all attacks are reported as soon as possible to the police to assist them in catching the attacker *before he strikes again*. Remember, the next victim may not be so lucky and may be killed.

It is very difficult for anyone to give a clear-cut ruling on how to deal with a rape situation, because attackers vary in age, height, weight, etc., and they also have different motives, e.g. sexual, anger, sadistic. The best advice I can give is initially always try to talk your way out of the situation in the hope that something you might say will help to nullify the attack and also gain you time for help to arrive. There are many reported cases where the victim talked a way out of the situation successfully and was able to walk away without being raped or physically harmed. Sometimes a prospective rapist needs help and just wants to talk to someone who is willing to listen. Sadly, this is not always the case, so other alternatives must be looked at.

How to talk your way out of a situation is important, e.g. if you feel that sexual gratification is the motive, attempt to thwart the attacker by saying you are on your monthly cycle, have a vaginal problem, are pregnant, etc.—anything that could deter him. If you know other people are close by who may hear you, shout 'Fire!': it seems to produce a better reaction than 'Rape!'

Physical defence should be used as a last resort, but having said that sometimes it is more advantageous to act first and ask questions later! By this I mean that as soon as an approach is made a quick reaction and strike at a vulnerable area could give you the advantage; sometimes delaying the response could be to your disadvantage.

Once again, it depends on the situation and individual cir-cumstances as to how you should deal with the aggressor. So, if you cannot talk your way out of the attack, then you have no alternative but to defend yourself in the most effective way possi-ble. You may not even have time to talk: you could be taken totally by surprise. In the photographs we have taken the situation to an advanced stage, i.e. the attacker already appears to have the advantage. The situation must now be reversed. (The ideal solution would, of course, have been to execute a technique *before* the attacker made his move. However, we are all taken off guard at some time and this instance is no exception.) Whenever you make your counter-attack, be positive in both your mental and physical approaches. Your attacker may be twice your size, but remember we all have vulnerable areas and can feel pain, so aim well and inflict the maximum damage at the exposed vital points.

Rape in the home

Attack from behind
Here a woman is at home, polishing. She has left the French doors open for a little fresh air and is unaware that the attacker has entered the room. By the time she realises what is happening, the attacker has made a grab from behind and has pulled her down viciously by her hair (photograph 1).

Being attacked while feeling safe in the comfort of your own home is a particularly horrifying experience. The victim here is taken very much by surprise and so she does not think to use the spray polish to her advantage – she could have sprayed into the attacker's eyes to give her chance to get away. The attacker forcefully grabs her hair and pulls her down to the floor.

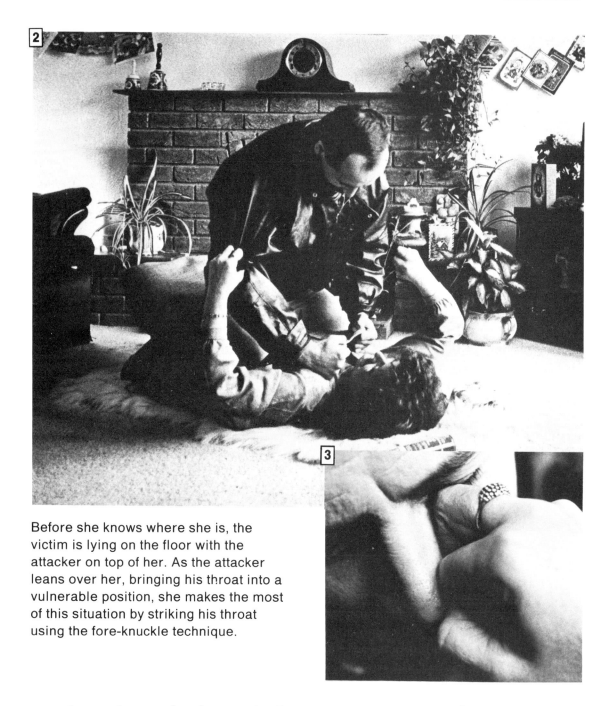

Before she knows where she is, the victim is lying on the floor with the attacker on top of her. As the attacker leans over her, bringing his throat into a vulnerable position, she makes the most of this situation by striking his throat using the fore-knuckle technique.

The attacker pins her down to the floor with his body weight and starts to rip off her blouse. This is where the victim can take advantage of her predicament, because the attacker has had to release his grip to remove her clothing. She strikes with her knuckles to the attacker's eye (see photographs 2 and 3). (Thumbs and fingers could be used here.)

Striking at the attacker's eyes with fingers would be a good alternative here.

As the attacker releases his grip to bring his hand up to his eye (photograph 4), the victim again seizes the opportunity to do a follow-up strike (punch) to the groin area while simultaneously making a grab for the throat with the left hand. Remember, it is not important which hand you use: it depends entirely on which makes it easier for you to execute the technique effectively. Also, as the attacker is in a state of arousal, his genitals will be prominent, making it easier for the victim to strike and cause the most amount of pain. The victim must execute a full length strike for maximum impact.

If you are unfortunate enough to be in a similar situation, remember that you have *teeth* and that they can be a very effective weapon, if you come into close contact with the attacker. Should the attacker hit you, do not deter: concentrate the pain you feel into anger. This will make you stronger and more determined to strike and get away.

Once you have caused enough pain to make the attacker release and you have given him something to think about, use the valuable time to follow up with a more effective finishing technique to give you a chance to get away and call for help.

While the attacker is distracted by the pain in his throat, the victim punches to his groin (grabbing and twisting are equally effective).

The throat grab is also important, because pressure is applied to vulnerable points, which causes more pain and so enables the victim to push the attacker to one side (photograph 5).

Note: calmness is a great advantage and helps the victim keep a clear mind.

In the photograph sequence the victim continues to push the attacker off and, as she starts to move away, she strikes with the elbow to his mandible (hinge between the skull and jaw bone).

Since the attacker is in pain from the two strikes, the victim is able to push him off and regain her freedom.

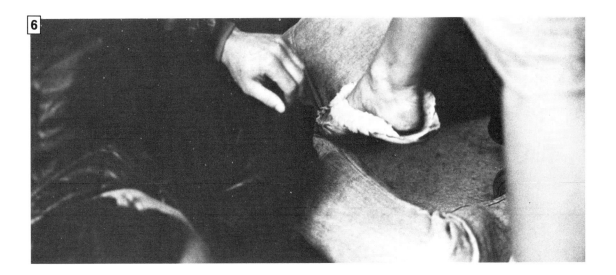

Alternatively, she could just stand straight up and do a final kick to the groin (photograph 6) or to the face area.

Once the attacker is immobilised, she should leave the house immediately and call the police (999): she may also need to call for an ambulance, depending upon how much damage she feels she has caused to her attacker.

She should not enter the house again on her own!

To make sure the rapist does not get up and try to continue with the assault the victim kicks once more to his groin.

Essential points to remember

Prevention is better than cure. To avoid finding yourself in a vulnerable situation, you can help yourself tremendously by taking a few simple precautions. Make sure your home is secure, don't bring strangers home or go into unknown places alone, and keep away from open waste land, desolate areas and alley ways. In other words, don't go anywhere that could be considered a high risk danger area. You may know of a good short cut to your home across open parkland or through a wooded area which takes 10 minutes off your journey, the usual route being through a busy street. I would definitely opt for the busy street every time. It would be a built-up area with plenty of people around, thereby reducing the risk of attack. Even practising martial artistes do not take unnecessary risks, or at least they should not. Have a sensible approach and use your common sense.

Unfortunately, even when all precautions and measures have been taken to prevent being a high risk casualty you can still become a victim of unforeseen circumstances and this is something no one can avoid. If you have to defend yourself physically it must not be half-hearted. Commit yourself one hundred per cent and strike with full aggression to your assailant's vulnerable areas.

7

DEFENCE AGAINST SEVERAL ATTACKERS

Multi-storey car park

Two attackers

Having dealt with a one-to-one situation, we can now look at how to cope with more than one opponent. If you are able to immobilise the first aggressor successfully, this should deter the others from following through with an attack. However, it is not always the case, so other methods of defence may have to be incorporated.

In the event of a multiple attack, do not restrict your vision just to one attacker. Try to have overall awareness so that you can detect movement and react in time to defend yourself from the first attack. If one of the attackers has a weapon, be particularly wary of him because initially he is the most dangerous. If one of the unarmed attackers moves in first, try to use a defensive technique which will cause him to act as a human shield against the attacker holding the weapon. Stepping back, if possible, while defending, will also assist in creating more distance between you and the attackers. Try to avoid stepping forwards nearer to the attackers.

Should the aggressor with the knife attack first and you successfully disarm him, do not allow the knife to get into the hands of the other attackers. Try to obtain the knife yourself so that you can use it to deter the other attackers from approaching you.

In this particular photograph sequence there are two attackers who want to steal a car and rob the owner of any money he may have. One of the attackers will be using a hammer in the assault. (Car parks are not attended on every floor so it is easy for attackers to conceal themselves and wait for a victim.)

The victim is collecting his car when the first attacker suddenly grabs him by his left shoulder with his right hand, with the intention of pulling the victim round to strike him (photograph 1).

An innocent victim goes to collect his car from a multi-storey car park and is seized from behind.

The victim swings his left arm round, over and under the attacker's arm to apply an arm-locking technique (see photographs 2 and 3). The victim simultaneously blocks a roundhouse punch coming in to his head with the knife edge of his hand (photograph 4). The victim then strikes with a hammer fist into the attacker's collar bone. Again, the strike could vary to the mandible, side of the throat, or temple, or, alternatively, he could strike using the knife edge of his hand to the temple. In fact, any hard technique to the face could be utilised here: see chapter 1.

The victim immediately applies an arm lever, placing his left arm over the attacker's right arm.

A close-up of the arm lock. Note: an arm lock must be applied at the elbow joint, or just above it, for maximum effect.

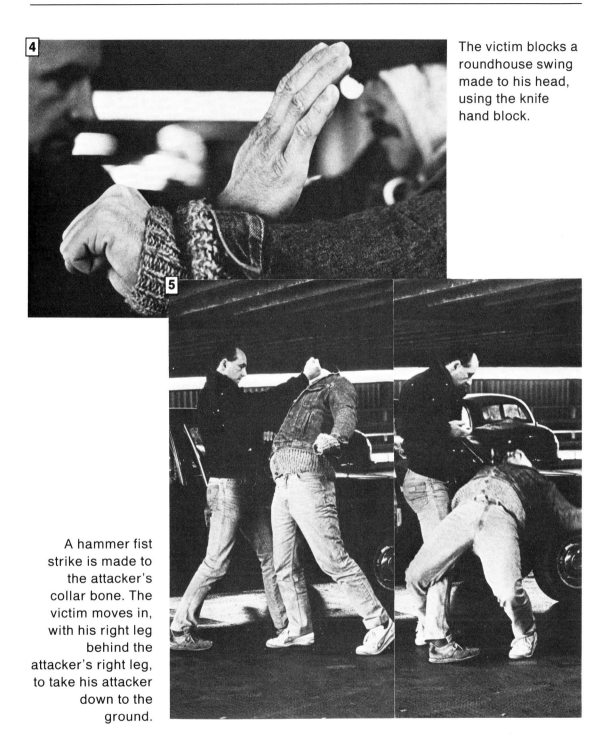

The victim blocks a roundhouse swing made to his head, using the knife hand block.

A hammer fist strike is made to the attacker's collar bone. The victim moves in, with his right leg behind the attacker's right leg, to take his attacker down to the ground.

The victim uses a 'take-down' technique, by placing his right leg behind the attacker's right leg, to put his assailant off-balance (photograph 5). The victim then executes a final punch to one of the attacker's vulnerable areas, e.g. floating rib.

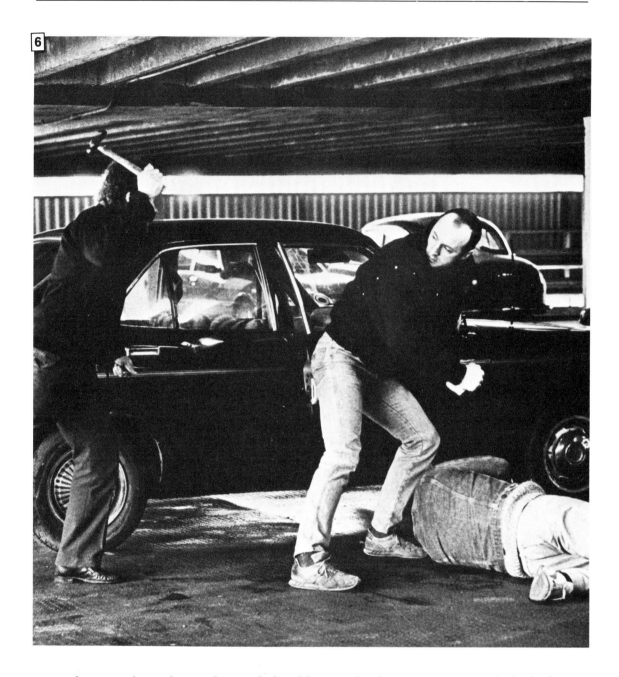

The second attacker rushes up behind him with a hammer in his right hand, with the intention of hitting the victim on top of the head (photograph 6). However, the victim uses a rising block (outer forearm block) to stop the attack (photograph 7). This is followed by an elbow strike to the point of the chin and is coupled with a leg-sweeping technique to take the second attacker down to the floor (photograph 8).

Again, a final punch is executed, this time to the temple.

The victim looks round to make sure he is now safe. As he does so, he sees a second attacker rushing at him with a hammer.

A close-up of the block used to deflect the hammer attack.

This time the victim executes an uppercut elbow strike to the attacker's chin and then follows through with a leg sweep.

Subway or underpass

Three attackers

Unfortunately, underpasses and subways are quite notorious for attacks, both during the day and at night. The following example incorporates three attackers.

The attack has been pre-arranged so that the victim will be completely surrounded, i.e. one will walk behind to prevent her running back, and the other two will conceal themselves in front of the subway exit (photograph 1).

The unsuspecting victim is walking into danger.

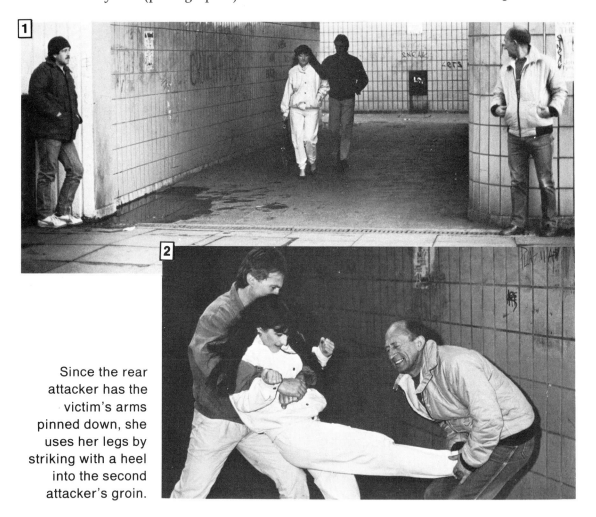

Since the rear attacker has the victim's arms pinned down, she uses her legs by striking with a heel into the second attacker's groin.

The first attacker runs up and grabs her from behind in a bear-hug hold, pinning her arms down. Therefore, she only has her legs at this stage to use in defending herself against the second attacker. The second attacker moves in and she kicks him in the groin (photograph 2).

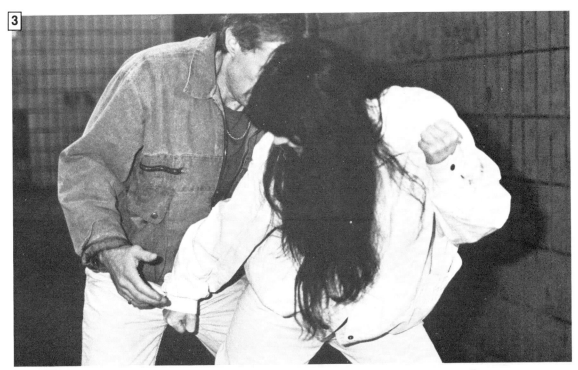

She strikes in hammer fashion to the first attacker's groin, which causes him to release his grip and he falls in pain (photograph 3). The third attacker makes a grab for her right wrist with his left hand (photograph 4). She then applies the principle of the

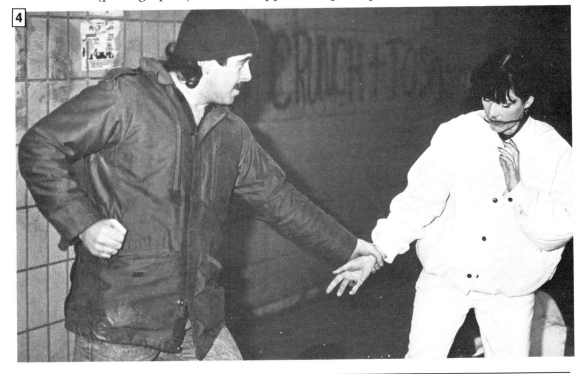

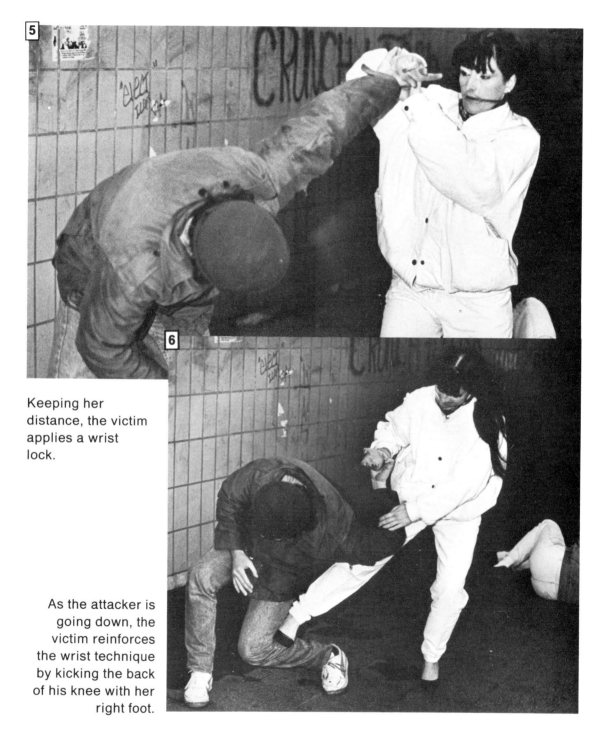

5

6

Keeping her distance, the victim applies a wrist lock.

As the attacker is going down, the victim reinforces the wrist technique by kicking the back of his knee with her right foot.

circle to disengage the grip and simultaneously strikes with the knife edge of her foot to the back of the third attacker's knee (photographs 5 and 6). This causes him to fall to the ground where she applies a final punch to his head.

8
CONFINED AREAS

Many attacks take place in confined areas, such as a lift, lobby, hallway or crowded room. This immediately means that movements and manoeuvrability are restricted. Minimum resources have to be used to maximum advantage, e.g. execute short, direct movements or apply techniques on pressure points.

In the next attack we see the victim inside the lift with just one attacker. Again, it could happen during the day or night, when going to or from work, while shopping, or in a hotel, etc. Whatever the situation, the victim is totally aware that the other occupant of the lift has intentions of attacking her. As the lift moves he immediately grabs her around the throat and pushes her up against the lift wall. She is unable to run; screams are unlikely to be heard or, if they are, it will be difficult, if not impossible, for anyone to come to her aid, so she has to rely totally on her own resources. Timing is essential. From the initial grab, the attacker could decide to punch the victim to incapacitate her. Before this happens, she must immediately strike to the attacker's most exposed vulnerable areas.

A variety of different techniques will be shown which could be applied in this sort of situation.

Front attack

The attacker has seized the victim and has pinned her up against the lift wall (see photograph below). She could execute a number of techniques from this position, as follows:

Being attacked in a confined space with nowhere to run is a very frightening experience. Here the attacker roughly grabs the victim's clothing and pushes her up against the lift wall.

(a) knuckle strike to the throat;

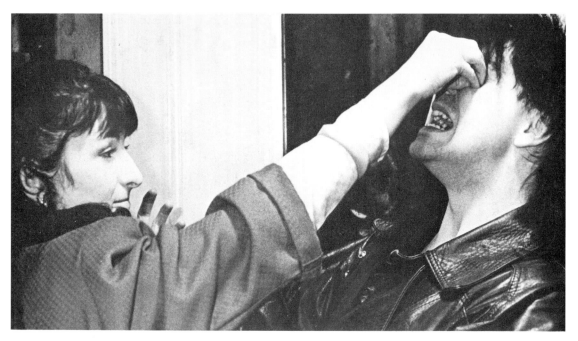

(b) chicken beak to the eye by pinching the fingers together into the shape of a bird's beak;

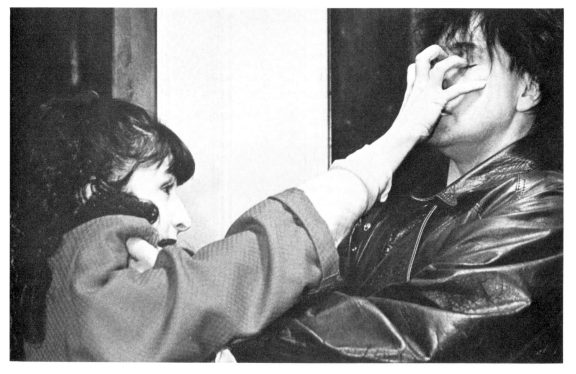

(c) fingers to the face, catching the eyes in the process;

(d) hammer fist to the nose;

(e) elbow to the nose;

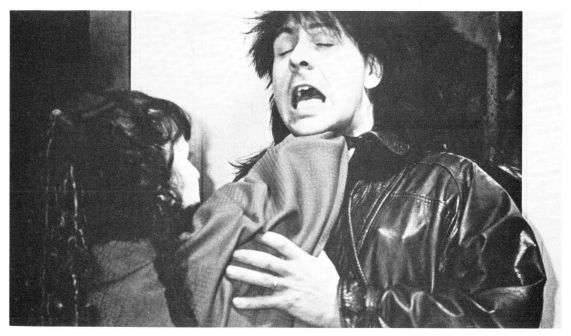

(f) elbow to the chin (any elbow strike would be effective here);

(g) palm heel to the nose;

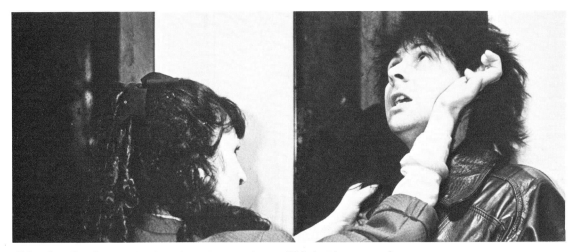

(h)   knife edge of the hand to the jaw (mandible). The *second stage* of the defence could be as follows:

A very effective strike to the groin using the ridge of the hand in an upward sweeping motion. The victim aims through the groin area up to the attacker's waist.

(a)   to apply a restraining technique to take the attacker down to the floor, or to follow up with a hard technique, such as:

(b)   to strike with a ridge hand to the groin; or

(c)   to strike with the knee to the groin, pulling the attacker down onto the knee for maximum impact.

Attack from behind (strangle hold)

The attacker grabs the victim around the throat and pulls her back. The victim can execute a variety of techniques, such as the following:

(a) the aggressor has not taken hold of the victim's other arm so she can use this to strike with the elbow to his solar plexus (in the photograph below she is assisting movement of her left elbow with her right hand);

Note: the victim is enhancing her left elbow strike by assisting with her right hand.

(b) she could apply a hammer fist to the groin; or,

(c) she could use both techniques together, i.e. strike with the elbow and, as the attacker releases his hold, follow up with the hammer fist to the groin.

Another variation after the initial self-defence technique is to spin round and strike the elbow into the nose, pulling the assailant's head onto the attack by grabbing his hair or ears. This again gives more impact to the technique. Alternatively, just seizing the back of the head and pulling downwards can be successful.

Variation on the rear attack

The victim uses a stamping technique by striking her stilettoes down the attacker's shin. She could follow through with either:

(a) fingers to the face;

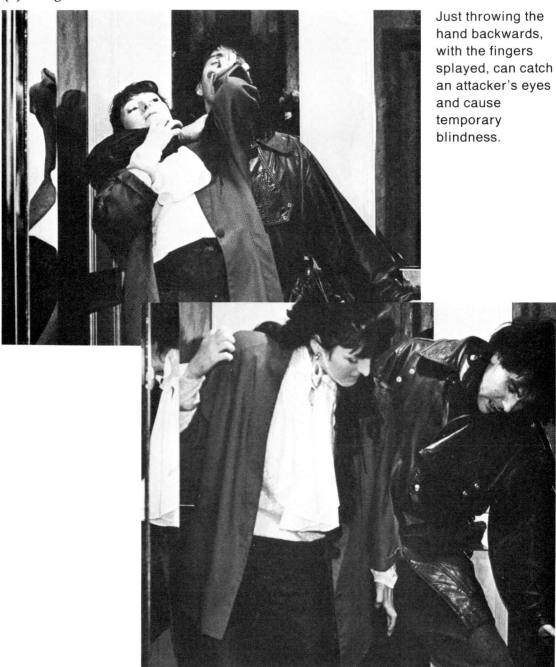

Just throwing the hand backwards, with the fingers splayed, can catch an attacker's eyes and cause temporary blindness.

(b) a knife-hand strike to the groin;

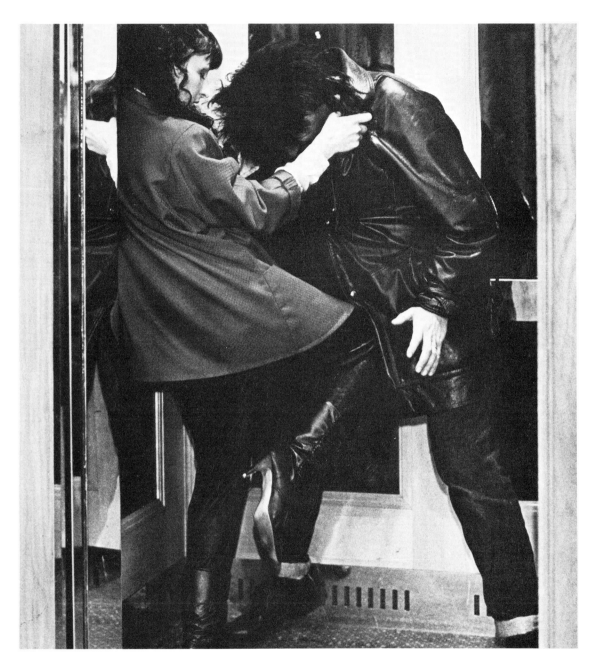

(c) knee to the face; or

(d) knee to the groin.

Although her attacker may have fallen down, she must still show awareness until the lift doors open and she can get away safely.

As she has nowhere to run, the victim makes sure she fully incapacitates the attacker by executing a knee strike to his groin.

LEGAL ASPECTS

In law you are allowed the right to defend yourself or loved ones when being attacked by using 'reasonable restraint'; otherwise, it is possible that the victim could end up being the party sued for grievous bodily harm. It is up to the victim to prove to the court of law that it was a self-defence situation and that there was no alternative. However, it is very difficult to define 'reasonable restraint', especially in the heat of the moment when your life or that of a loved one is seriously threatened. In a life and death situation it is advisable to immobilise the attacker in the best way possible and to sort out the consequences later. The law does not permit violence on provocation, only on a physical assault.

If you find yourself in a dangerous situation from which you can only effectively defend yourself by using a weapon, such as a knife, try to strike to the attacker's leg or arm area; the pain should be enough to deter him, giving you time to get away. If you aim to the body and seriously injure or kill the attacker, you could be penalised for manslaughter – again, this would depend on the jury believing it was a self-defence situation.

The police, in particular, are at an immediate disadvantage, because they must avoid inflicting any physical harm while carrying out their duties. This, of course, also applies to anyone in a similar employment, including nurses who may be attacked by patients.

As already mentioned, talking your way out of the situation is the best course of action. Failing this, if you have to resort to physical defensive measures, do not be deluded into thinking you are exempt from prosecution yourself. Be aware of your legal position: you have to prove your case. The only reward is knowing you are still in one piece to be able to do this!

To clarify the point a little further, let's take an example and see how it would be viewed legally.

In chapter 5, where a burglar has intruded onto private property and has attacked the occupier (in this case it is a senior citizen, but it could be a housewife, teenager, etc.), the victim has reacted quite naturally by defending himself in the best way possible with his walking stick against the burglar. If the burglar had been hurt badly he could have taken action against the elderly man for inflicting injury, even though he himself would face prosecution for burglary. However, in this example only three techniques were applied. They were sufficient to incapacitate the burglar and give the victim time to get away and call for help. Therefore, a court of law would probably rule that the senior citizen did use 'reasonable restraint' and his case would be dismissed.

If, on the other hand, the victim had not only hit the burglar on the nose and in the groin, but had also kicked him repeatedly, when he was lying on the floor, on the head or chest, and had caused extensive external and, perhaps, internal injuries, then this would, of course, be seen as 'unreasonable' behaviour. A court of law would no doubt conclude that excessive, unnecessary force, rather than 'reasonable restraint', had been used.

Similar criteria apply to any self-defence situation in which the victim retaliates to such an extent that serious injury is inflicted on the potential mugger, burglar or rapist. Even after the car park incident, described in chapter 7, in which the victim has dealt successfully with a number of attackers, the victim should get in his car and should go to the nearest telephone box or police station to report the incident. He should not continue with gratuitous violence, such as breaking the arm of the attacker who is lying on the floor. Furthermore, even though a burglar may be contravening the law by intruding onto private property, an owner has no legal right to shoot him, causing wounding or death.

To summarise: the main objective in self defence is to incapacitate an attacker and there will be occasions, as shown throughout the book, when more than one technique is required. Once you are satisfied that the attacker has received enough damage to prevent him from continuing with the assault, no further injury should be inflicted.

It can be argued that in the heat of the moment a victim blinded by fear does not necessarily realise just how excessive his retaliation may be, but this is why each case is given careful consideration. Always be prepared and remember your legal rights. Do not think you can brutally beat up a mugger, even if you feel he deserves it; be careful and use common sense.

CONCLUSION

All the events portrayed throughout this book are constructions of possible atttacks to give a general idea of how self-defence techniques can be applied *in situ*. No on can say this is exactly what would happen, but it does help to be able to see the practical application of techniques in realistic situations and surroundings.

The basic idea is to adapt the knowledge and application of such techniques to your own personal advantage. Linked with this must always be a correct mental approach and the confidence to carry out manoeuvres. The essence of self defence is to try to deflect in a positive manner the force coming towards you, no matter how much stronger, physically, the opponent may appear. You must never think the situation is impossible and you do not stand a chance – have a go! We all have vulnerable areas, no matter how heavy, tall or strong we are.

So, breaking everything down, what I am saying is be *positive*, have confidence in yourself and your ability, know your own strengths and weaknesses, try talking your way out of a situation first, and if this fails focus maximum force and energy on your opponent's vulnerable areas. Do not feel intimidated and always use common sense. Utilise your own body as an effective weapon and if you are fairly small in stature make body movement and speed your asset against a heavier foe.

Important points to remember

1   Always use discretion and common sense when dealing with a difficult situation and when choosing defence techniques. If the aggressor is a friend or a relative you certainly do not want to do him any harm or permanent injury. Therefore, a restraining technique would be more appropriate. However, if the aggressor carries a knife and is intent on severe physical violence, even on killing, then a positive technique to immobilise him until help arrives would be the best course of action.

2   Always assume the aggressor is dangerous; never underestimate him. Be prepared for anyone and anything.

3   Although confidence is important, never be over-confident to the point of confusing your thoughts.

4   Always aim at the attacker's vulnerable areas. Never waste time and energy in striking the hard muscle areas where no damage or little damage can be done.

5   Use your body as a complete unit for maximum power. Hip momentum and good posture also help to enhance the strength of your technique (although this may be restricted in senior citizens).

6   Use skirting techniques and evasive action when blocking an attack, if at all possible, to harmonise with or ride the attacker's force. If the aggressor is superior in weight and build, you can utilise his force to your advantage. By diverting the attack you can place yourself in a better position for a counter-attack.

7   Never be afraid to do something out of the ordinary to distract or unbalance the aggressor to give you the advantage or to deter him from continuing with the assault. The element of surprise can be an advantage.

8   A strong foundation is important to execute an effective technique, so make sure you have good mobility. This will obviously vary for individuals who are elderly, may be confined to a wheel chair, are disabled, or are unable to utilise hip momentum (due to arthritis, for example).

9   Always try to talk your way out of a situation and use physical defence as a last resort. Do not provoke a situation unnecessarily.

10   Be aware of your legal position and do not inflict unnecessary injury once you are completely satisfied the aggressor is safely immobilised.

11   Report all incidents to the police, no matter how trivial you feel the attack may have been.

MARTIAL ARTS CLUBS

If you would like to take self defence further, I would suggest making enquiries about local reputable self-defence or martial arts clubs in your area. There are many different arts and styles from which to choose, all of which have something important to offer if you have a good instructor and you are a willing student. I feel it is wrong to say that one art is better than another. Also, different arts suit different individuals and what may suit one person may not suit another. By trying various arts you should be able to find one you like. Decide whether you want to perfect an art, which requires years of practice and dedication, or whether you just want to learn a very basic self-defence system. Below is a list of some well-known arts, with brief outlines of their basic principles.

Karate
This art utilises the body's own force and momentum against the opponent. Basic punching and kicking and a strong stance are the main attributes of the art. Techniques vary according to the style of karate (there are various systems of karate which originate from different parts of Japan; although they may look very similar, there are basic differences in stance, in the application of forms (set movements), and in terminology).

Kung fu
This is similar to karate, but has different stances, application of techniques and posture. Terminology also varies, as the art originates from China.

Aikido
In aikido the defender utilises the principle of the circle to harmonise with the opponent's force. It does not matter how strong the opponent is because, by employing pure technique, the defender will use all the opponent's strength against him.

Judo
Judo is based on the point of balance. The opponent's posture is broken and he is thrown to the floor, after which a restraining technique is applied. This art is now widely acknowledged as an exciting sport in the Olympic Games.

Jujitsu

This art is based on throwing techniques, arm locks and strangle holds. Various techniques used in jujitsu can also be found in aikido and judo.

Shinto ryu

It is a combination of all the above arts and has a broader scope for the martial arts practitioner who wants a wide choice of defence techniques: either hard techniques or harmonising with an opponent's force can be used.

For an effective self-defence system I feel that all the main principles should be learned so that an individual can use and adapt techniques that are the most appropriate for him and for the situation. A combination art like shinto ryu is suitable for all ages and can cater for the many different situations which may arise.

USEFUL HINTS

General

☐ If attacked, make a full commitment to defend yourself. Be positive: aim to survive!

☐ Awareness and aggression are key factors in a self-defence situation. We all possess these qualities, so don't be afraid to use them. Be aware of danger areas and take steps to avoid them.

☐ Use techniques that are natural and comfortable for you. Elaborate techniques are not always the most effective techniques!

☐ Use a weapon as a last resort, but once you have committed yourself do not back down – the weapon could be used against you!

☐ Look at a potentially aggressive situation realistically and try to calm down people if at all possible.

☐ Do not wash if you have been attacked or raped. You may be carrying vital evidence which will assist the police in trying to track down your attacker.

☐ When going into an unknown environment, be cautious and check the area carefully. For example, if going into a public convenience, check all the cubicles first, but make sure that you don't look as though you're behaving suspiciously!

☐ Women and girls who like to keep their nails fairly long may find these useful as self-defence weapons!

Home

☐ Secure good locks to doors and windows, and fit a spy hole to your front door. Fit chains to front and back doors. (Locks fitted to bedroom doors may be useful, but do not let children use them in case they need your help during the night.)

☐ An alarm is a good deterrent if you can afford one.

☐ Avoid letting strangers into your home, especially if you are on your own. Many people tend to leave back doors open, particularly during the summer, but whenever you are alone you should lock doors (and perhaps downstairs windows if you are going upstairs for a bath).

Work

☐ Avoid going into unknown areas on your own, especially if

there is access for the general public and you are some distance from work colleagues.

☐ Personal alarms are becoming popular. If you are walking out and about alone, carry your personal alarm in your hand – it is of no use to you in a bag if you need to use it quickly.

☐ If a work colleague begins to harrass you, use diplomacy and tact to defuse the situation. Avoid verbal, or physical, abuse.

Car

☐ Always lock your car when you leave it, no matter how quick you think you will be. It takes only a minute for someone to climb in the back.

☐ If you are sitting in a car alone, lock all doors and avoid winding down the window if you are unsure of a situation or a stranger is approaching.

☐ Do not pick up strangers. Do not accept lifts from strangers.

Public transport

☐ Be careful at night. Travel with a friend and, if possible, avoid sitting upstairs on a double-decker bus.

☐ The underground is particularly dangerous at night, so try to avoid using it at this time.

☐ Use a reputable taxi service – budget your night out to include this because it's money well spent.

Streets

☐ If you are walking home, especially at night, avoid underpasses/subways. Keep to well-lit built-up areas.

☐ In your defence use whatever is to hand, e.g. stick, pencil, book, bag, umbrella, hair spray.

☐ Do not rely on other people to come to your rescue. You must have faith in your own ability. Remember: you have nothing to lose in trying.

Note

Biting an attacker can be an effective deterrent in certain circumstances, but it is suggested that readers be aware of the facts concerning AIDS before deciding whether to incorporate this technique into their self-defence repertoire.

INDEX